Francis Frith's
Nothumberland

Photographic Memories

Francis Frith's
Northumberland

Maureen Anderson

FRITH
BOOK Co

First published in the United Kingdom in 2002 by
Frith Book Company Ltd

Hardback Edition 2002
ISBN 1-85937-522-7

British Library Cataloguing in Publication Data

Francis Frith's Northumberland
Maureen Anderson

Frith Book Company Ltd
Frith's Barn, Teffont,
Salisbury, Wiltshire SP3 5QP
Tel: +44 (0) 1722 716 376
Email: info@francisfrith.co.uk
www.francisfrith.co.uk

Printed and bound in Great Britain

Front Cover: Seahouses, The Harbour c1955 S521027

Contents

Francis Frith: *Victorian Pioneer*

FRANCIS FRITH, Victorian founder of the world-famous photographic archive, was a complex and multi-talented man. A devout Quaker and a highly successful Victorian businessman, he was both philosophic by nature and pioneering in outlook.

By 1855 Francis Frith had already established a wholesale grocery business in Liverpool, and sold it for the astonishing sum of £200,000, which is the equivalent today of over £15,000,000. Now a multi-millionaire, he was able to indulge his passion for travel. As a child he had pored over travel books written by early explorers, and his fancy and imagination had been stirred by family holidays to the sublime mountain regions of Wales and Scotland. 'What a land of spirit-stirring and enriching scenes and places!' he had written. He was to return to these scenes of grandeur in later years to 'recapture the thousands of vivid and tender memories', but with a different purpose. Now in his thirties, and captivated by the new science of photography, Frith set out on a series of pioneering journeys to the Nile regions that occupied him from 1856 until 1860.

Intrigue and Adventure

He took with him on his travels a specially-designed wicker carriage that acted as both dark-room and sleeping chamber. These far-flung journeys were packed with intrigue and adventure. In his life story, written when he was sixty-three, Frith tells of being held captive by bandits, and of fighting 'an awful midnight battle to the very point of surrender with a deadly pack of hungry, wild dogs'. Sporting flowing Arab costume, Frith arrived at Akaba by camel seventy years before Lawrence, where he encountered 'desert princes and rival sheikhs, blazing with jewel-hilted swords'.

During these extraordinary adventures he was assiduously exploring the desert regions bordering the Nile and patiently recording the antiquities and peoples with his camera. He was the first photographer to venture beyond the sixth cataract. Africa was still the mysterious 'Dark Continent', and Stanley and Livingstone's historic meeting was a decade into the future. The conditions for picture taking confound belief. He laboured for hours in his wicker dark-room in the sweltering heat of the desert, while the volatile chemicals fizzed dangerously in their trays. Often he was forced to work in remote tombs and caves where conditions were cooler. Back in London he exhibited his photographs and was 'rapturously cheered' by members of the Royal Society. His reputation as a photographer was made overnight. An eminent modern historian has likened their impact on the population of the time to that on our own generation of the first photographs taken on the surface of the moon.

Venture of a Life-Time

Characteristically, Frith quickly spotted the opportunity to create a new business as a specialist publisher of photographs. He lived in an era of immense and sometimes violent change. For the poor in the early part of Victoria's reign work was a drudge and the hours long, and people had precious little free time to enjoy themselves. Most had no transport other than a cart or gig at their disposal, and had not travelled far beyond the boundaries of their own town or village. However,

by the 1870s, the railways had threaded their way across the country, and Bank Holidays and half-day Saturdays had been made obligatory by Act of Parliament. All of a sudden the ordinary working man and his family were able to enjoy days out and see a little more of the world.

With characteristic business acumen, Francis Frith foresaw that these new tourists would enjoy having souvenirs to commemorate their days out. In 1860 he married Mary Ann Rosling and set out with the intention of photographing every city, town and village in Britain. For the next thirty years he travelled the country by train and by pony and trap, producing fine photographs of seaside resorts and beauty spots that were keenly bought by millions of Victorians. These prints were painstakingly pasted into family albums and pored over during the dark nights of winter, rekindling precious memories of summer excursions.

The Rise of Frith & Co

Frith's studio was soon supplying retail shops all over the country. To meet the demand he gathered about him a small team of photographers, and published the work of independent artist-photographers of the calibre of Roger Fenton and Francis Bedford. In order to gain some understanding of the scale of Frith's business one only has to look at the catalogue issued by Frith & Co in 1886: it runs to some 670 pages, listing not only many thousands of views of the British Isles but also many photographs of most European countries, and China, Japan, the USA and Canada – note the sample page shown above from the hand-written *Frith & Co* ledgers detailing pictures taken. By 1890 Frith had created the greatest specialist photographic publishing company in the world,

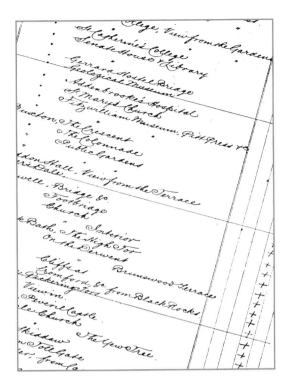

with over 2,000 outlets – more than the combined number that Boots and W H Smith have today! The picture on the right shows the *Frith & Co* display board at Ingleton in the Yorkshire Dales. Beautifully constructed with mahogany frame and gilt inserts, it could display up to a dozen local scenes.

Postcard Bonanza

The ever-popular holiday postcard we know today took many years to develop. In 1870 the Post Office issued the first plain cards, with a pre-printed stamp on one face. In 1894 they allowed other publishers' cards to be sent through the mail with an attached adhesive halfpenny stamp. Demand grew rapidly, and in 1895 a new size of postcard was permitted called the court card, but there was little room for illustration. In 1899, a year after

Frith's death, a new card measuring 5.5 x 3.5 inches became the standard format, but it was not until 1902 that the divided back came into being, with address and message on one face and a full-size illustration on the other. *Frith & Co* were in the vanguard of postcard development, and Frith's sons Eustace and Cyril continued their father's monumental task, expanding the number of views offered to the public and recording more and more places in Britain, as the coasts and countryside were opened up to mass travel.

Francis Frith died in 1898 at his villa in Cannes, his great project still growing. The archive he created continued in business for another seventy years. By 1970 it contained over a third of a million pictures of 7,000 cities, towns and villages. The massive photographic record Frith has left to us stands as a living monument to a special and very remarkable man.

Frith's Archive: *A Unique Legacy*

FRANCIS FRITH'S legacy to us today is of immense significance and value, for the magnificent archive of evocative photographs he created provides a unique record of change in 7,000 cities, towns and villages throughout Britain over a century and more. Frith and his fellow studio photographers revisited locations many times down the years to update their views, compiling for us an enthralling and colourful pageant of British life and character.

We tend to think of Frith's sepia views of Britain as nostalgic, for most of us use them to conjure up memories of places in our own lives with which we have family associations. It often makes us forget that to Francis Frith they were records of daily life as it was actually being lived in the cities, towns and villages of his day. The Victorian age was one of great and often bewildering change for ordinary people, and though the pictures evoke an impression of slower times, life was as busy and hectic as it is today.

We are fortunate that Frith was a photographer of the people, dedicated to recording the minutiae of everyday life. For it is this sheer wealth of visual data, the painstaking chronicle of changes in dress, transport, street layouts, buildings, housing, engineering and landscape that captivates us so much today. His remarkable images offer us a powerful link with the past and with the lives of our ancestors.

Today's Technology

Computers have now made it possible for Frith's many thousands of images to be accessed almost instantly. In the Frith archive today, each photograph is carefully 'digitised' then stored on a CD Rom. Frith archivists can locate a single photograph amongst thousands within seconds. Views can be catalogued and sorted under a variety of categories of place and content to the immediate benefit of researchers.

Inexpensive reference prints can be created for them at the touch of a mouse button, and a wide range of books and other printed materials assembled and published for a wider, more general readership - in the next twelve months over a hundred Frith local history titles will be published! The day-to-day workings of the archive are very different from how they were in Francis Frith's time: imagine the herculean task of sorting through eleven tons of glass negatives as Frith had to do to locate a particular sequence of pictures! Yet

See Frith at www.francisfrith.co.uk

the archive still prides itself on maintaining the same high standards of excellence laid down by Francis Frith, including the painstaking cataloguing and indexing of every view.

It is curious to reflect on how the internet now allows researchers in America and elsewhere greater instant access to the archive than Frith himself ever enjoyed. Many thousands of individual views can be called up on screen within seconds on one of the Frith internet sites, enabling people living continents away to revisit the streets of their ancestral home town, or view places in Britain where they have enjoyed holidays. Many overseas researchers welcome the chance to view special theme selections, such as transport, sports, costume and ancient monuments.

We are certain that Francis Frith would have heartily approved of these modern developments in imaging techniques, for he himself was always working at the very limits of Victorian photographic technology.

The Value of the Archive Today

Because of the benefits brought by the computer, Frith's images are increasingly studied by social historians, by researchers into genealogy and ancestory, by architects, town planners, and by teachers and schoolchildren involved in local history projects.

In addition, the archive offers every one of us an opportunity to examine the places where we and our families have lived and worked down the years. Highly successful in Frith's own era, the archive is now, a century and more on, entering a new phase of popularity.

The Past in Tune with the Future

Historians consider the Francis Frith Collection to be of prime national importance. It is the only archive of its kind remaining in private ownership and has been valued at a million pounds. However, this figure is now rapidly increasing as digital technology enables more and more people around the world to enjoy its benefits.

Francis Frith's archive is now housed in an historic timber barn in the beautiful village of Teffont in Wiltshire. Its founder would not recognize the archive office as it is today. In place of the many thousands of dusty boxes containing glass plate negatives and an all-pervading odour of photographic chemicals, there are now ranks of computer screens. He would be amazed to watch his images travelling round the world at unimaginable speeds through network and internet lines.

The archive's future is both bright and exciting. Francis Frith, with his unshakeable belief in making photographs available to the greatest number of people, would undoubtedly approve of what is being done today with his lifetime's work. His photographs, depicting our shared past, are now bringing pleasure and enlightenment to millions around the world a century and more after his death.

Northumberland - *An Introduction*

FRITH CAMERAMEN TOOK relatively few photographs in the 19th century of what is now the county of Northumberland. Perhaps this was because the county was not such a large tourist attraction at the time, and the views would not have sold as postcards in large quantities. There are some early images here, but most date from 1950 to 1965, just as changes to industry and the way in which people made their living were coming about.

Known as the 'cradle of Christianity' because of the connections with St Aidan and St Cuthbert, the area has a strong religious history. It has also seen many bloody raids and Border battles. With the breakdown of the Roman Empire, the Saxons and Vikings invaded the country. Then after the Norman Conquest castles were built to protect the coast from further invasion; although this kept the peace to some extent, the Border battles continued for centuries until Scotland and England became united under one crown.

Evidence of our ancestors is to be seen all over the county. Some of this evidence, in the form of burial cairns, cup and ring marks in the rocks, stone circles and hill forts, is believed to be from as long ago as 5,000 years. Other relics include mighty castles, pele towers, monasteries, churches and the great wall built by Hadrian.

Once stretching from Strathclyde to the Humber, Northumbria's geographical borders have diminished over the centuries, but the county still covers a vast area. There are 60 miles of changing coastline and nearly 400 square miles of National Park with its hills and wooded valleys, and in the North Pennines, named an Area of Outstanding

Natural Beauty, there are moorlands and charming, ancient stone-built villages. The Great Whin Sill was formed by a kind of basalt being forced underground between layers of rock during the volcanic era. This dramatic natural formation stretches from Upper Teesdale in the west to the Farne Islands in the east. Hadrian used the inland cliffs to build parts of his defensive wall. Changes in the landscape that were not formed by nature include Kielder Water and forest, which is the largest man-made lake and forest in Western Europe.

Industry has played a strong part in the shaping of the area. Deep mining for coal was once important: during the Industrial Revolution, Northumberland was the biggest supplier. The Pennines was a source of lead. The development of the mines meant that houses had to be built to accommodate the workers and their families, and so towns sprang up. The scars left by mining have nearly all been reclaimed by nature now, but the heritage lives on in the many museums that depict the way of life of the mining families.

The county has been the birthplace of many of England's famous sons and daughters. As well as Aidan and Cuthbert, there was King Edwin, who built the most northern city of Northumbria, Edwin's Burgh, later to become Edinburgh. Lancelot 'Capability' Brown, the master of landscape gardening, received the nickname Capability from his saying that a place had capabilities. Admiral Lord Collingwood was Nelson's second-in-command at the Battle of Trafalgar. Dorothy Forster was involved in the Jacobite rebellion. George Stephenson was dubbed 'Father of the Railways'; and Grace Darling, the lifeboat heroine who died in 1842 of tuberculosis, was buried in Bamburgh churchyard. A museum opposite the churchyard commemorates her bravery in 1838 when she and her father rowed a boat from the Longstone lighthouse through a severe storm to rescue nine people from a floundering ship.

Agriculture developed in the 18th and 19th centuries. Today a large part of the county is still given to agriculture, with sheep farming and forestry foremost. Many of the market towns still prosper, the focal point for the surrounding farming communities. Because the farmers rely heavily on livestock for their living, the recent foot and mouth outbreak had a devastating effect on their livelihoods. In turn this affected the towns and villages, and the tourists coming into the area. While this catastrophe will not be forgotten for many years to come, in true Northumbrian spirit the people are fighting back and are regaining their hold on the land and tourism.

The Coast

From just north of Berwick-on-Tweed to Tynemouth stretch miles of virtually unspoilt coastline. The waves of the unpredictable North Sea pound against rugged cliffs, wash gently onto the sandy beaches of the sheltered bays and lap against the moored boats of the coastal villages. Once, fishing was the livelihood of many. An annual event for the fishermen with their small boats was to follow the shoals of herring during their summer migration as they moved from the Northern Isles down the east coast of Scotland and into the waters of Northumberland. The fisher girls or 'fish wives', experts at gutting and curing the fish, would also follow the shoals. But the fishing declined here as it did all over Britain, and the people had to turn their hands to other means of making a living. Beside the sailing skills of the fishermen, seamanship was also evident in the many volunteer lifeboat crews that rescued hundreds, if not thousands, of otherwise doomed sailors.

Towards the end of the Victorian era, rail travel had brought about greater mobility for the working classes. People who worked in the cramped factories of the smog-filled towns yearned for open countryside and beaches. Thus the villages that once relied upon fishing for their income began catering for visitors. As the 20th century dawned, fishermen's cottages and small lodging houses gave way to large hotels, and many of the fishermen's boats began to be used to take visitors on sightseeing trips or fishing excursions. Harbours that were once commercial, transporting coal, lime, grain and other commodities, were spruced up and became moorings for pleasure craft. The abundance of wildlife, the beautiful coastline and the historic relics brought the visitors flocking in their thousands.

The fishing industry still carries on in some of the coastal towns and villages, but on a much smaller scale than 100 years ago. Now many of them are quiet resorts used by tourists as a base from which to visit other places nearby. Others treble their population in the summer months - an example is Seahouses, where trips can be made to the Farne Islands. Besides their religious significance, these islands are also unique sanctuaries that are home or breeding grounds to thousands of seabirds and seals. The largest of the islands is Inner Farne, the home of St Cuthbert in 696. A church built there in 1370 was dedicated to him, and is open to the public. The Holy Island of Lindisfarne can be reached by a causeway when the tide is low, but is cut off from the mainland at high tide.

Another bird sanctuary is at Coquet Island, which is protected by the RSPB. Boat trips to the island can be taken from Amble, said to be 'the friendliest port'. Newton-by-the-Sea has a sheltered bay which is ideal for water sports, and nearby Craster provides the famous Craster kippers, as well as harvesting lobsters and crabs from the whinstone platform that juts out into the sea.

In contrast to the fishing industry, the village of Beadnell boasts well-preserved limekilns. These date from the 18th and 19th centuries, when lime was quarried near the village and then exported from the little harbour. The wide sweep of Beadnell bay stretches from the harbour to Snook and Newton Points. Embleton Bay is another wide, long sweep of beautiful beach overlooked by the brooding ruins of Dunstanburgh Castle.

History, solitude and relaxation can be found along this magnificent coast by anyone who enjoys being close to nature.

Seaton Sluice
The Harbour c1955 S523010
Part of the old village of Hartley, this area once flourished with the glass trade and coal. Sir Ralph Delaval transformed the small natural harbour in the 17th century; sluice gates were installed and piers built. Now a quiet resort, the harbour is used as moorings by fishing and sightseeing boats.

**Seaton Sluice
The Memorial c1940**
S523006
The houses to the right were once known as Irish Row because of the Irish miners who lived there. Behind the houses is the Watch House with its little belfry, which belongs to the lifesavers established in 1876 with 25 volunteers. The memorial still stands on the green, but the railings were removed for munitions for the war effort.

**Newbiggin-by-the-Sea
Sandy Bay Caravan Site
c1960** N76067
Sad to say, industry is a blot on many otherwise beautiful landscapes, and here the power station at Blyth is no exception. Of course the up side to this is that industry supplies our modern-day conveniences and employment. This caravan park still caters for visitors in the summer months.

Newbiggin-by-the-Sea The Bay c1960 N76040
In the distance, on a headland away from the village, stands the church of St Bartholomew - it has an extremely interesting 13th-century interior. Looking at this view, it is hard to believe that this was once an important lead-mining area.

Newbiggin-by-the-Sea, The Promenade c1960 N76062
At the turn of the century this was a popular resort, with visitors arriving daily in the summer by train. An old red phone box stands outside the post office to the left. Two children are enjoying ice cream, while the older generation sit on the benches or lean on the wall to look out at the sea.

Newbiggin-by-the-Sea, Front Street c1965 N76080
Many families, mainly from Newcastle, had holiday homes overlooking the beautiful bay. Over the years some of the bay has collapsed, possibly owing to the lead mine workings. In recent years much has been done to restore the town. Behind the bus shelter tarmac is being laid. On the right are Lloyds Bank, amusements, the New Dolphin Hotel and a BP garage.

Cresswell
The Beach c1955 C460019
The family sitting amongst the sand dunes seems to have finished their picnic. A box, a magazine and a beach ball have been abandoned. Further along the dunes a group of bikes are parked while their owners follow other pursuits. Although plenty of people are on the beach, no one has ventured into the sea. Perhaps the water is too cold!

Cresswell, The Village c1960 C460035
The little shop in the centre was the sub-post office that eventually moved premises - the shop now sells souvenirs. The larger shop on the right once sold groceries, but it now sells ice cream and drinks. The view from these buildings must have been superb, with the wide sweep of Druridge Bay on one side and horses grazing peacefully on the other.

Amble, The Pier c1965 A225053
The harbour was built in the 19th century when Amble was prosperous as a centre for the export of coal. Now it is popular for leisure sailing, and has a large marina. While families take in the fresh air, another man relaxes and gazes out at the view, and a fisherman patiently waits for a nibble.

Amble, Queen Street c1960 A225038
This was once a small village; the streets developed along with the harbour in the 1830s. To the left, a lady inspects the wares laid out in the window of the Co-operative stores.

◄ **Alnmouth
General View c1955**
A222036
During the storm of 1806, the village church was destroyed. The Duke of Northumberland converted a granary into a temporary church. We can see the spire of the new church, that was built in 1876, rising above the houses.

Alnmouth, The River Aln c1965 A222033

Alnmouth was once a very successful port. But a violent storm in 1806 caused the river to break through and form a channel cutting off Church Hill from the village. Because the new channel was not so deep as the old one, large sailing vessels could no longer use it, and the port went into decline.

Alnmouth, Main Street c1955 A222076

Alnmouth dates back to the early days of Christianity, and was an important port in medieval times. Because of its beautiful sands, the village is now a peaceful resort. The harbour is a popular mooring for inshore fishing boats and pleasure craft. A nearby golf course also attracts visitors.

Longhoughton Lowstead Beach c1960 L320014

A road through a farm leads from the village to this beautiful beach known as Sugar Sands Bay. In the village, the vicarage and the church of St Peter and St Paul were reputed to have been used by smugglers from Boulmer in the 17th and 18th centuries.

▼ **Craster, The Harbour 1951** C352001

About a mile from here is the 15th-century Craster Tower, owned by the family that gave the village its name. The family's roots in the area date back to the Norman Conquest. Most of the houses are constructed with the whinstone that the village stands upon.

▼ **Craster, The Harbour 1964** C352060

Herrings were once caught locally, but they are now brought in from north-west Scotland. The kipper factory was established at the turn of the century, and it is there that the raw fish are taken. In a process than can take up to sixteen hours, the end product is the oak-smoked kippers for which Craster is renowned.

▲ **Embleton**
The Beach and the
Castle c1960 E150034
The beautiful bay has a splendid view of the ruins of Dunstanburgh Castle, on the cliff top to the east. There is no road to the castle, but it can be reached by a leisurely stroll of about two miles along these sands.

◀ **Embleton**
The Golf Clubhouse and the Links c1960 E150044
James Braid founded this course in 1900. In 1947 the Men's Club was founded. Since its beginnings, the course has gone from strength to strength. With views over Embleton Bay and the castle, this is a very scenic course.

Newton-by-the-Sea
The Village c1965 N202023
In the 18th century, fishing was the main livelihood here.
The area now belongs to the National Trust. A lady toils up
the incline with her bag of shopping, past the coastguard
station. Many buildings like this one are now used as
holiday cottages in the summer months.

Newton-by-the-Sea, Beach Square c1965 N202016
This part of the village is known as Newton Seahouses or Low Newton. These fishermen's cottages make up three sides of a square that faces out to sea. These and the two-storey Ship Inn in the centre are 18th-century, although it is thought that parts of the inn are much earlier.

Beadnell, From Swinhoe Road c1955 B550021
The earliest record of the village dates from 1161. Agriculture was once the mainstay of the economy, with corn being taken to the harbour to be shipped out. This view at the edge of the village shows the vast expanse of arable land. Limestone quarrying was also an industry carried out here in the 18th and 19th centuries.

**Beadnell
The Harbour and the
Shore c1960** B550044
Herring fishing and
curing became the main
source of income in the
19th century. As with
many fishing
communities around
Britain, the local
fishermen could not
afford the larger boats
that were needed to
travel longer distances in
the quest for fish, and
the industry declined.
The few that still make
their living from the sea
rely on catches of crabs,
lobsters, trout and
salmon.

Seahouses, Sunrise c1955 S521028
Steam drifters took over from the smaller fishing boats at the end of the 19th and beginning of the 20th century in most of the coastal towns and villages. Seahouses managed to hang on to their sailing boats until the 1920s, when motor driven drifters began to be used. In this dawn view a steamer is coming in towards the harbour.

**Seahouses
The Harbour c1955**
S521093
A view of a busy day at the harbour. A large tank is visible by the sea wall (centre). The small crowd is probably waiting to be taken out to sea on a sightseeing tour. One of the boats to the rear is the 'Seahouses', and BK 30 at the front is named 'Faithful.'

Seahouses
The Harbour c1955 S521027
This village grew up in 1889, when the harbour was built to
improve the fishing industry in the area. We can see signs
of this industry in this charming view - crab and lobster pots are
stacked on the pier, and the premises of Dawson's, the fish
salesman, are beside the sea wall, centre left.

Bamburgh, Eider Duck c1935 B547023a
Guillemots, terns, razorbills, puffins and eider ducks are some of the wild species of birds that use the Farne Islands as their breeding grounds from mid May to mid July. The noise is unbelievable, and the mess even worse. But for anyone who is a keen birdwatcher, the attraction is obvious.

Farne Island, Herring Gull Stealing a Gannet's Eggs c1960 F152024
The mother gannet had probably gone in search of food herself and left the nest unattended, so the cheeky seagull has sneaked onto the nest to steal its dinner. Gulls are scavengers - and where better to find food than these islands in the breeding season.

**Farne Island
Grey Atlantic Seals c1960**
F152017
The Longstone lighthouse stands silent guard over the wild terrain and its inhabitants. The island is the home to around 4,000 grey seals, a protected species here; they breed at the rate of about one thousand seal pups a year. This seal community is one of earth's treasures - let us hope that it will not become extinct.

**Holy Island
The Causeway c1955**
H348160
Out of every twenty-four hours there are up to eleven when the island is cut off from the mainland. At low tide the island is surrounded by a vast expanse of sand on which thousands of wild birds feed. The sign states that it is 'one and three quarter miles over sands at end of causeway'.

◄ Holy Island
Post Office Green c1930
H348099

When the south wind blows, the market cross has been known to fall down. The sign on the old post office advertises 'Robert Bell Provision Merchant. Motor Cars and Conveyances for Hire'. The smart car and the cart are perhaps two of his 'conveyances'. The building is now a private residence.

**Holy Island
A Pleasure Boat
c1935** H348133
The boatman stands in the centre with his boathook, while his passengers pose for the camera. They certainly look as though they are all enjoying themselves. On the stern of the boat a small flagpole displays a Red Ensign.

Towns, Villages and the Countryside

The Viking raids and the Border wars have left echoes of an ancient and bloody past that can be seen in the many relics that remain all over this vast county. The Emperor Hadrian built Hadrian's Wall between Bowness on the Solway Firth and Wallsend on the Tyne in 122 AD. The wall was originally about 73 miles long and 5 metres high, and was built to keep the land of the Britons separate from that of the Picts. Hadrian's Wall attracts millions of visitors annually, and brings welcome revenue to the towns and villages that are near to the surviving parts of the wall. Corbridge was on the main Roman route from Scotland to York, and the many historical remains show that it must have been a substantial town. It was also the supply base for the troops that were stationed on the wall, as the well-preserved granaries testify. Ruins of Roman forts also survive along the wall. Chesters fort by the side of the Tyne is the best preserved of them all, and contains a bathhouse. Housesteads fort is the most complete, containing latrines and a hospital.

The Cheviot Hills stand as a rampart between Scotland and England. For centuries the Border Reivers raided the towns and villages for their cattle and sheep. Now the grassy tracks that once echoed to the shouts of bandits and sounds of livestock being driven to market by the drovers are used by walkers. The peaceful grasslands at the northern part of the Northumberland National Park are dotted with grazing Cheviot sheep. Byrness, on the Pennine Way, is the last village before the crossing at Carter Bar into Scotland. This point in upper Redesdale was the scene of an affray in 1575 between the English and the Scots. The irony of this was that it began because of an argument between the two peacekeepers about their respective sides of the border. The Warden of the English Marches and the Keeper of Liddlesdale met under what was supposed to be a truce; but tempers flared, and what was supposed to be a peaceful meeting turned into a battle.

Many of the towns and villages suffered badly in the Border raids. Bellingham was an important market town and a rich source of plunder, and was constantly being raided. Wark was the capital of North Tynedale, and its castle was of great importance as a Border fortress. Because of this, it was regularly under attack; today nothing much remains except the large mound, or motte, where this formidable building once stood. In Blanchland the abbey was badly damaged by fire, and many of the monks were killed by the raiders.

Some of what were once small hamlets saw rapid growth as coal mining settlements, such as Ashington, Acomb and Haltwhistle. Haltwhistle is now the largest town in South Tynedale, and the closest to Hadrian's Wall. Allendale was a former lead-mining settlement, and has a strong case for its claim to being the geographical centre of Britain.

Alnwick, in the shadow of its castle, grew as a busy commercial centre from 1291 when it received its first market charter. The town's medieval past is re-enacted every year during the Alnwick Fair. Hexham was also a busy market town; the market place, which is centuries old, still sets up stalls in front of St Wilfred's abbey. Modern shops jostle for space alongside old buildings on its narrow, hilly, twisting streets. Whether we visit the attractive towns and villages or the hills, forest and wild moorland that surround them, the history of our ancestors fighting for the land is always only one step behind.

Allenheads
The Falls, Dovespool c1955 A221016
The River Allen joins the South Tyne in a Pennine valley. Only four miles or so upstream it merges with the larger rivers of the East and West Allen. At the sides of the rivers, natural pools form; these were often adapted for man's use, perhaps for sheep dipping or for children to bathe.

▼ Allenheads, The Village c1955 A221029

Situated at the head of the twisting East Allen valley, this was once an important lead-mining centre. The village has an irregular square and a chapel, as well as a scattering of cottages. The memorial is to those who died in the Great War, and has a small piece by S R W Milburn inscribed upon it.

▼ Blanchland, The Square c1955 B555078

The post office is in the castellated building to the rear of the square. To the right is the Lord Crewe Arms. Some of the building dates from the 12th century, and some from 17th-century alterations. The ghost of Dorothy Forster, sister to Tom Forster who led the Jacobite uprising in 1715, is said to haunt the hotel to this day.

▲ Blanchland
The Village c1965
B555082
The name of this charming village is derived from Norman French, and means 'the white-lands'. This could have related to the white habits of the monks of the abbey that was founded here in 1165. Most of the houses are built with stone from the old abbey, and date from around 1752.

◄ **Allendale, Aerial View c1955** A102080
Allendale was once a busy lead-mining centre, and the buildings, mainly constructed with local grey-brown stone, date mainly from the 18th and 19th centuries when the industry was at its peak. Mining must have been thirsty work - there were a great number of inns and hotels around the market place.

**Gilsland ▶
The Cross,
Bewcastle 1924**
76663
The 7th-century
cross stands 4.4m
tall, and is thought to
have been carved for
the Anglian King
Alchfrith. It has
wonderful carvings of
biblical figures on
one side, and
animals, trees, fruit
and birds decorate
the others. The
church was dedicated
to St Cuthbert, and
was built in the time
of Edward I.

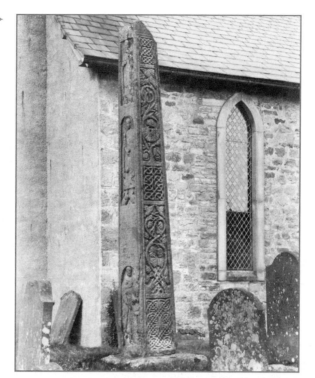

▼ **Gilsland, The Vicarage, Roman Altars and Stones 1924** 76660
Some sections of Hadrian's Wall were narrow, and some were built
with turf because of a shortage of stone. Here, in a former vicarage
garden south of the centre of Gilsland village, about 220 yards of the
wall was built on a wide base to conserve the stone.

▲ **Gilsland, Roman Wall
Crag Lough 1924** 76662
This impressive lough is
situated beneath the cliffs
of Whin Sill, giving
dramatic views to the
walkers following the
Wall. For rock climbing
enthusiasts, this area is
the best in
Northumberland.

Bardon Mill, The Roman Wall at Winshields Crag and Crag Lough c1960
B548004
This is the highest point of Hadrian's Wall at 345m. The Roman fort of Vindolanda stands between here and Once Brewed. The lookout and signalling post on the crest of Windshields commanded a vast uninterrupted view, but it would have been extremely windy.

**Haydon Bridge
The Village c1950**
H345012
A lovely view of the
village, overlooking the
stone bridge that has
been much altered
since it was constructed
in 1773. Towards the
left is the clock tower of
St Cuthbert's church; it
was built in 1796 using
the materials from a
previous church.

◄ **Acomb**
The Green c1955
A250003
Once a coal mining community, the village is now in two parts. This is the old part, which comprises mainly 18th-century houses built round a very pretty square. The manor house dates from 1736, and the church from 1875. The village is now mainly used by Tyneside commuters.

Newbrough, The Stores
c1955 N201001

Opposite the pretty cottages is the general store, with its lone Esso petrol pump outside. This was a common sight until safety regulations for combustible fuels were brought in. These stores are also almost a thing of the past now, as supermarkets with their cheaper mass-produced goods spring up everywhere. At the end of the road is parked what might perhaps be a school bus.

Corbridge, Devil's Water Dilston Falls c1955 C459008

These falls were not only easy on the eye but were also serviceable. When the nearby watermill was in use, after powering the waterwheel, the tailrace came over Devil's Water on an aqueduct to drive another waterwheel, which then powered a threshing machine at Dilston Haugh Farm.

Corbridge Corstopitum c1955
C459012

These are the impressive ruins of a Roman fort that was built by Julius Agricola in about AD 80 to guard an important crossing on the River Tyne. It was later used as a very important military supply base for Hadrian's Wall. To the right in the distance, the seven-arched bridge of 1674 spans the Tyne.

◀ **Wylam**
From the North c1950
W397001
To the rear of the view
we can see the tower of
St Oswin's church.
George Hedley, son of
the railway pioneer
William Hedley,
dedicated the church to
the village in 1886.
Dozens of neatly-kept
allotments are spread
out along the north bank
of the Tyne, in front of
the village.

Stocksfield
The Railway Station
c1955 S520008

The station was such a distance from the village that horse-drawn cabs were used to meet the trains. The railway cottages, to the bottom left of the view, were all demolished in 1969. The building in the centre was an inn in the 19th century and early 20th century, and is now a private residence.

Wylam, Main Street c1955
W397009

Wylam's claim to fame is that it was the real birthplace of the railways. William Hedley built his Puffing Billy to haul coal from Wylam colliery to Lemington Staithes. George Stephenson, another railway pioneer, was born here. The sign for the Ship, which is still a hotel, hangs above the doorway on the left of the view.

Wark, The Green and the Memorial
c1960 W393025

The memorial commemorates the men who died in the Great War. This village was once part of the estates of the earls of Derwentwater. It passed into the hands of the Commissioners of Greenwich Hospital in the early 18th century. The tree in the centre of the little green is a fine old chestnut.

**Byrness
Catcleugh Reservoir
c1960** B557005
This artificial lake was
completed in 1905 to
supply extra water for
Tyneside. Hundreds of
navvies were employed
in its construction, and
horses and carts
removed all the debris.
Some people are making
the most of the lake by
sailing a little boat.

**Rochester, Byrness
Forestry Village c1965**
R316017
The Forestry Commission
built many of the rather
uniform houses in the
village for their
employees and their
families. The village
church has a stained
glass window in memory
of those who died while
building the nearby
Catcleugh Reservoir.

Rochester, Carter Bar c1955 R316020
A little tea wagon is parked just over the Scottish border on the A68 to Jedburgh. This Cheviot viewpoint looks towards the Cheviot Hills, which stretch for 45 kilometres from Carter Bar to Yetholme Mains. The sign reads 'County of Roxburgh, Jedburgh 11 miles, Newcastle 47 miles'.

Otterburn, England from Carter Bar c1955

084024

The village of Otterburn is almost in the centre of the National Park amid wild and rugged moorland. The name 'Carter' comes from the Celtic word 'cart', meaning 'hill', and 'Bar' comes from the tollhouse that stood here when the turnpike was built in the 18th century. The sheep do not seem to expect any traffic on the road.

▼ **Bellingham, High Street c1960** B552019

19th-century greystone buildings dominate this ancient capital of the North Tyne Valley. On the left are the town hall and its clock. A sign for K Shoes juts out from a shop front, while next door a woman appears to be looking into a shop window.

▼ **Bellingham, Hareshaw Lynn c1955** B552001

This beautiful waterfall, cascading about 30 feet, is situated in a peaceful wooded glen, just a short walk from the village. Another water source is Cuddy's Well, which is reputed to have healing properties. The story arises from St Cuthbert's body being laid in the church while the monks were seeking a final resting place for him.

▲ **West Woodburn General View c1955**

W394024

Situated in the deep valley of the Rede, the village is near the old Roman route from York to Scotland and one of the Roman outpost forts. In the valley also stands the 11th-century Corsenside church, which is dedicated to St Cuthbert.

◄ Humshaugh, The Village c1965 H349011
A few of the buildings here date from the 17th century, but most of the older ones are from 1816. Many of the houses in nearby Haughton were demolished in that year to make way for the castle park, and houses were built in Humshaugh to re-house some of the families. The church of St Peter, centre left, was built about 1818.

▼ **Wall, The Green c1955** W392016
The buildings grouped around the large square green are mainly
17th-century. The Methodist chapel and reading room, centre right,
are 19th-century. At one time the green was probably enclosed so
that animals could be driven in and kept safe at night from raiders.

▼ **Ashington, Station Road c1960** A224028
When a coal seam was found in about 1867, nearby Ashington began
as a pit village. As the population grew, so did the need for shops,
schools and public buildings. Station Road became the main shopping
street; the council chambers and clock tower were built in about 1910.

▲ **Ashington, Milburn
Road c1955** A224022a
There are a few billboards
decorating this store on
the corner of Fifth
Avenue and Milburn
Road. The logo of Walter
Willson's proclaims that it
is a 'Smiling Service
Shop'. The company was
to later drop one of the
Ls to become Wilson. A
little girl in a white dress
is either trying to post a
letter or to peek through
the post box slot.

Ashington, Station Road c1960 A224015
The town once boasted five cinemas, but one by one they all closed. The Wallaw, pictured on the right, was the last to go in 1982. One cinema, the Pavilion, became a bingo hall. Station Road is now pedestrians only, and is a pleasant shopping precinct.

◄ **Bedlington
Front Street West
c1955** B551010
Development of the town began in the 1840s with the sinking of the first coal mine in the area. The town's claim to fame is the breed of dog that originated in the area. In the late 19th century, the breed was known as the Rothbury terrier; it then became the Bedlington terrier, named after the town of its birth.

◄ Ashington, The Park
c1955 A224032
The statue is in memory of the miners who died in the Woodhorn Colliery explosion in 1916; it has a dedication and a sketch of a colliery engraved on its plinth. It is now part of the Woodhorn Colliery Museum, once a working pit. The buildings, situated near Queen Elizabeth II Park, opened as a museum in 1989.

▼ Bedlington, Humford Mill the Stepping Stones c1960
B551030
The attractions of this country park are five miles of woodland walks that follow the River Blyth and horse riding trails. What a perfect setting for a weekend picnic. Besides the beautiful scenery, the park also has barbecues and a paddling pool for the children set in a clearing at Humford Mill.

◄ Warkworth Market Place c1965
W391026
The market cross in the centre is c1830, and its base is even older. To the right is the Warkworth branch of the Amble Co-op store. The Norman church of St Laurence peeps out over the trees, and a gentleman standing in the road, in front of the Mason's Arms, poses for the camera.

▼ Warkworth, Castle Street c1960 W391029

The Hermitage Inn on the left was built in the early 18th century. The windows are segment-headed, and there is brickwork behind the rendering. A single-decker bus wends its way past a parked open-backed truck towards Warkworth Castle. Behind the fountain is the Castle Garage.

▼ Mitford, The Village c1955 M254004

Towards the bottom of the hill is the Plough Inn; it was rebuilt in brick when the earlier stone building succumbed to fire in the 1930s. Opposite is Cartwright's timber yard. The Brown family owned this for over a hundred years until the 1970s. The land is now a housing development.

▲ Alnwick, Bondgate Within c1955 A223023

Barclay's Bank is to the far right of the view. On the fork of the cobbled street, with its copper dome rising above the trees, is a building that has been known by different names, including Red Stamp Corner. Further along is the clock tower of the town hall, originally built in 1736 as a tollbooth and guardhouse.

◄ **Thropton, The Village
c1955** T227008
Pretty stone cottages line
both sides of the street.
Thropton Tower, which was
a 15th-century pele tower
(a tower built in defence
against border raids), has
been converted into a
house. A billboard,
advertising Senior Service
cigarettes, decorates the
wall of a car hire firm.

◀ **Rothbury
General View c1955**
R360043
Rothbury Bridge leads into this pleasant town. The square tower of All Saints church is to the left of the view. Sad to say, the church was almost completely rebuilt in 1850 and little of the medieval parts survive. From the 18th century a market developed for the cattle and sheep for Upper Coquetdale, and the town became busy catering for drovers and tradesmen.

◀ **Thropton, Simonside c1960** T227025
The holidaymakers with their caravans and little tent certainly have an unobstructed view of the countryside. Obviously they are not concerned about the legends of the little people that are supposed to live amongst the crags around here.

▼ **Whittingham The Fountain c1955** W395001
Known as the Ravensworth Fountain, this is situated at the foot of the village green. It was designed by George Reavell, and erected in 1905. The statue is of the Earl of Ravensworth, the local landowner, and his dog. The house behind the fountain has pretty leaded windows to the upper storey.

◀ **Glanton, The Village c1950** G212006
A grocer's delivery van collects goods from Smith and Clark. These were once a common sight going door to door, especially in rural areas. A 'clean sweep' is held here every year, where everyone cleans a small area of the village. There is also an annual show that has been held since the beginning of the 20th century.

▼ **Chatton, The Village c1955** C454007
This village is part of the Duke of Northumberland's estates. The
buildings are mainly mid 19th century. There are two once very
common sights in this view: to the left is an old-style red telephone box,
and to the right is a lone petrol pump just outside one of the cottages.

▼ **Harbottle, The Fountain c1960** H246006
The Victorian Gothic fountain was by Macmillan of Alnwick, and it was
erected in 1880. This is the main village of upper Coquetdale, and the
attractive houses are mainly of stone. The Star Inn on the left now
caters for tourists and walkers as well as the local people.

▲ **Harbottle
General View c1960**
H246035
To the left we can see
part of the ruins of
Harbottle Castle. It was
built in 1106 by the
medieval barons of
Redesdale. In the 17th
century much of the
stonework was removed
to build the houses in the
village.

◄ **Wooler, Happy Valley c1960** W396006
This beautiful stream, Colgate Burn, is also known as Wooler Water; it is a tributary of the River Till. The Till is formed by the confluence of the Harthorpe and Carey burns that rise in the Cheviot Hills.

**Wooler, Skirl Naked
c1955** W396003
Cyclists and ramblers
regularly use these trails
that take them through
the Harthorpe Valley to
the Cheviot Hills. This
stream is known as
Carey Burn. Many of
the places in
Northumberland have
quaint names such as
Skirl Naked, Pity Me
and Blaw Wearie.

◀ **Branxton, The Village c1955** B556005
This peaceful scene belies the fact that near the village stands a plain granite cross that marks the battle of Flodden Field. Here the English defeated the Scots in a bloody and violent battle in September 1513. It was the last battle to be fought on English soil between the Scots and the English.

Belford, High Street
c1955 B553050
This was once an important town on the Great North Road used by armies and stagecoaches. On the far left is the 18th-century coaching inn, the Blue Bell, which now serves tourists as a hotel. The pinnacles and lancet windows of St Mary's church rise above the buildings.

Ford, The Village c1950
F207002
Ford was owned by the Heron family, and Etal by the Manners family. In the 14th century there was bitter disputes between them. The twin villages overlooking the Till valley were not united until in the 20th century, when Baron Joicey, a mine owner from Durham, bought Ford in 1907 and Etal in 1908.

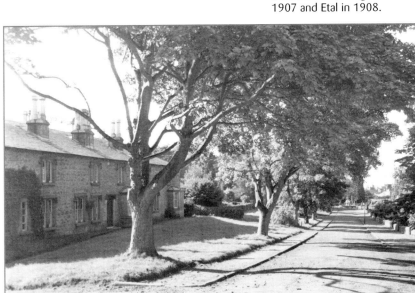

Lowick, The Village
c1955 L321006
To the right is a 17th-century inn, the Black Bull. The small building with the sloping roof has now gone, and the inn is painted white, making this view look very different now. The other hotel in the village is the White Swan.

Lowick
The Memorial c1955 L321005
This view of Main Street looks west towards the crossroads, with
the war memorial to the right. The small building has now gone,
changing this view somewhat. The area was once known for its
lime production, and some of the wagon ways used to transport
the lime have been incorporated into bridleways.

Churches, Rivers and Bridges

The many rivers and their tributaries that flow through Northumberland give rise to some of the wildest and most spectacular scenery in Britain. The Tyne rises from the highest point of the Pennines not far from the source of the River Tees. Berwick-upon-Tweed, the most northerly town in England, sits on the mouth of the River Tweed. Other rivers such as the Rede, the Till, the Aln and the Wansbeck snake their way through the landscape. Smaller streams or burns are home to a multitude of wildlife, including otters. The larger rivers are well used by fishermen angling for sea-trout and salmon.

The bridges that span the rivers now echo to the sound of modern traffic. In ancient times the sound would have been the clip-clop of horses and the rattle of carts. Many of the very early crossings, especially if built from wood, were washed away in river floods. Some of the ancient bridges that remain are used as footbridges. Others have been strengthened to carry the heavy traffic of the present day, and sometimes new bridges have been built alongside the old, such as at Berwick-on-Tweed. The town has three bridges, one built in sandstone in the 17th century, the Royal Border 28-arch bridge built by Robert Stephenson in 1850, and the Royal Tweed completed in 1928.

King Oswald was a convert to Christianity. After spending some years in exile, he regained the throne of Northumbria. He sent for monks to spread the word of the gospel throughout his kingdom, and in 635 Oswald and Aidan founded the church at Bamburgh. Aidan became the first Bishop of Northumbria; he was noted as a worker and as an inspiring example to all his clergy. Oswald invited the monks of Iona to establish a priory on the Holy Island of Lindisfarne. One of the reasons for choosing the island was that it was cut off from the mainland for a large portion of the day, so it was seen as a retreat. The priory was one of the most important centres for Christian learning in Western Europe.

In 650 Cuthbert began his ministry in Melrose, Scotland. He eventually became Bishop of Lindisfarne, successor to Aidan. Eleven years after his death, Cuthbert's coffin was opened: his body had not deteriorated and he lay as if asleep, and so he was declared a saint. The causeway to the island became known as Pilgrim's Way because of the thousands of pilgrims that walked to the priory to pay homage to the saints. When the island was in danger of attack from the Vikings, the monks decided to move St Cuthbert's body. Many of the churches in Northumberland are dedicated to St Cuthbert, as it is believed that the monks rested at these sites as they travelled with his body for more than 100 years. Eventually they laid the saint's body to rest at Dunholm, now the cathedral city of Durham. St Cuthbert's way, which is used by walkers, spans 63 miles of country from Melrose to Holy Island.

After St Cuthbert's death, St Wilfred was his successor, and the priory developed under him. During his reign the magnificent Lindisfarne gospels were written and decorated. St Wilfred's abbey in Hexham dates from 674. The oldest surviving part of the building is the Saxon crypt, which is similar to the crypt in York minster, which was also founded by the saint. St Wilfred's chair, well over 1,000 years old, is reputed to have been the coronation chair for the Northumbrian kings. It was also used as a sanctuary stool - the law could not touch any criminal who took refuge in the abbey and sat on the stool. It is thought that St Wilfred also founded a church at Bywell in the 7th century, although all that now remains is a carved stone. Almost every town and village has at least one church, and they all have their niche in the religious history of the county.

◄ **Blanchland**
The Church c1950
B555011
The Crewe trustees rebuilt the ruined monastic church of St Mary the Virgin in the 18th century. The restoration combined the 13th- and 14th-century remains into the repairs, resulting in an L-shaped building. To the right of the view is the Lord Crewe Arms, and in the centre is a 13th-century cross.

Haydon Bridge
The Bridge and the Reading Room
c1950 H345013
This six-arched bridge over the South Tyne was built in the 18th century; the arches are all of an unequal span. The north arch was rebuilt in 1969. A new road bridge was constructed in 1970 alongside the old one.

Prudhoe, The Old Chapel c1955 P265006
The square keep of Prudhoe Castle was built around 1175. Later, a moat, a drawbridge, a gatehouse and a chapel were built. The guardhouse and chapel are both reached by this outer staircase. The oriel window in the chapel is thought to be the finest and oldest in England.

Hexham, The Abbey 1888 21062
The abbey stands on the site of a much earlier church built by Wilfred in the 7th century. It is a mix of styles from medieval to the 20th century. Perhaps the most interesting part of the structure is the crypt. Built of Roman stones, it would probably have held relics that pilgrims would have viewed through grilles and by the light of oil lamps.

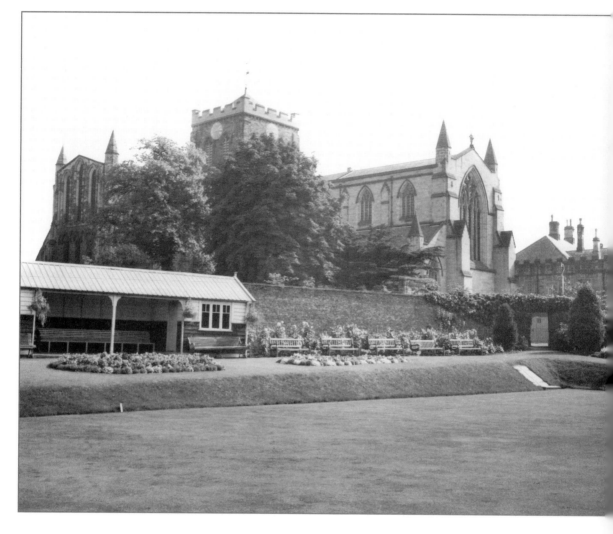

◀ **Hexham, The Bridge c1960** H80090
A seven-arch bridge over the River Tyne, was completed in 1770, but it was swept away in the great flood of 1771. Another bridge with nine arches was completed in 1782, but this was also destroyed in a severe storm in 1772. Eventually a famous architect, Robert Milne, was contracted to build another bridge. It was completed in 1793, and still stands today.

Hexham, The Abbey and the Bowling Green c1960 H80077

Dominating the skyline, the abbey stands in the centre of a busy market place and town, overlooking this well-manicured and beautifully landscaped park. It is an ideal place for a stroll at the end of a busy shopping day. The gardeners responsible for the park take great pride in keeping it looking at its very best.

▼ Bywell, The Bridge c1955 B860005

In the 19th century the villagers of Bywell were resettled in Stocksfield, and the village's buildings were removed for landscaping. This view is about a half mile from where the village once stood. The bridge over the wide river has five arches and a panelled parapet; it was built in 1838.

◄ Bywell, St Andrew's Church c1955 B860007

A small group of buildings remain in the area, despite the demolishing of the village. Amongst them are Bywell Hall, a castle and two ancient churches. The Saxon tower of this church is said to be the best in the country. Part of the church itself was altered almost beyond recognition in the 19th century.

▼ **Wylam, The Bridge c1965** W397019
Originally the superstructure of this bridge was of wood, built on stone piers. It was constructed in 1836 following the advent of the Newcastle and Carlisle Railway. Wagons would cross the bridge on their way to the iron works and Wylam Colliery on the north side.

▼ **Otterburn, The Rede and the Bridge c1955** O84006
The Scots and the English fought each other here in 1388 - the Scots were the victors. A stone column known as Percy's Cross stands just outside the village to mark the spot.

▲ **Bellingham, The Tyne and the Bridge c1955**
B552007
A bridge mentioned in the 12th century disappeared, and for centuries there was no bridge spanning the Tyne above Chollerford. The Newcastle architect, John Green, designed the present bridge, which was built in 1834.

◄ **Chollerton, St Giles's Church, Roman Pillars c1955** C456009
The exterior of the building is mainly 18th- and 19th-century. The interior tells a different story. This is 12th-century, and consists of an arcade of four bays. The monolithic Roman columns possibly came from Chester. A Roman altar dedicated to Jupiter that was found buried in the churchyard in the early 19th century is inverted and used as one of the fonts.

◄ **Ponteland, St Mary's Church c1955** P264028
The lower portions of the tower are Norman, and so is some of the interior. Alterations were carried out, beginning in the 13th century. The bell stage, the parapet and alterations to the chancel are 14th-century. Restoration work also took place in the 19th century. There is medieval stained glass to some of the windows.

◀ **Seaton Delaval The Church of Our Lady c1965** S522006
Originally this was the Delavals' manorial chapel. Some of the building dates from the early 12th century. The bellcote that we can see to the rear of the roof of the church is on the east nave gable - it is 19th-century. There are two effigies, one of a cross-legged knight and one of a lady.

▼ **Ponteland, The Bridge and the Diamond Inn c1965** P264004
Built in 1150, the sturdy tower of the church of St Mary the Virgin forms a backdrop to the bridge that spans the River Pont. To the side of the bridge, the Diamond Inn has changed little over the years. The area in front of the church, known as Coates Green, has been opened up and now forms a very pleasant area of parkland.

◀ **Bedlington Hartford Bridge c1960** B551020
The bridge was almost entirely rebuilt in 1904, but the north arch is of medieval origin. The house to the rear of the view is known as Hartford Bridge House; one of the outbuildings bears the date 1836.

▼ Bedlington, St Cuthbert's Church c1960 B551001
The church is mainly 12th-century, with 19th- and early 20th-century alterations. The village once came under Durham, and was the capital of Bedlingtonshire. It became a mining area when the first coal mine was sunk in 1840. There is a vicarage dating from 1835, and an 18th-century market cross.

▼ Morpeth, Telford Bridge c1955 M251049
Sometimes known as the New Bridge, this bridge was constructed between 1829 and 1831. An inscription on the parapet gives Thomas Telford as the designer. The cast iron lamps are the originals. The tall octagonal spire of St George's United Reformed church dominates the view at the end of the bridge.

▲ Morpeth, The River c1955 M251027
A little further upriver from the New Bridge a woman seems to be in tune with nature. There is no one about - except for the ducks, which are certainly interested in whatever titbits are being thrown to them. A latecomer is swimming as fast as it can to join in before its fellow ducks gobble all the treats.

Warkworth, The Bridge and the Tower c1960

W391032

In the 14th century, twenty marks were left by John Cook of Newcastle for the building of a bridge, and this was the outcome. At the south end, a tower was built, making this one of very few fortified bridges in England. Traffic now uses a modern road bridge to enter the village.

◄ **Lesbury, The Church c1965** L319009
Most of the exterior of St Mary's church was restored in the 19th century. The interior boasts some medieval features, but it is difficult to determine dates on all the remains. There is a 15th-century font with Percy emblems carved upon it. The landowner's emblems are also carved on some of the timbers.

Rothbury, The River Coquet from the Tennis Court c1955 R360022
Still a very pleasant place, the town was once a prosperous Victorian resort that was brought about with the coming of the railway. The Rothbury Bridge provides access from the south; it is a three-arched medieval bridge, and was strengthened in the 20th century with concrete and steel.

Alnwick, The Lion Bridge c1955 A223027
In 1770 a flood damaged the previous bridge over this part of the Aln. This bridge was built a little further up the river in 1773 - John Adam was the architect. Embattled parapets decorate the structure, along with the distinctive lion, made of cast lead, which gives the bridge its title.

Alnwick, The Castle and the Lion Bridge c1955 A223001
In 1309 Henry de Percy purchased the castle and added to it. The fourth de Percy became an earl, and eleven more followed him. When the male line died out, Lady Elizabeth Seymour, the heiress, married Sir Hugh Seymour. He became the first Duke of Northumberland, and he took the family name so that the Percy line would continue.

▼ Chatton, Holy Cross Church c1955 C454004

This church was built in 1770. Salvin added the north aisle in 1846, and in 1897 the roof to the tower was altered and the windows were gothicized. Some medieval cross slab memorials are built into the floor of the baptistery. The reredos dates from 1895, and is the work of Arthur Moore.

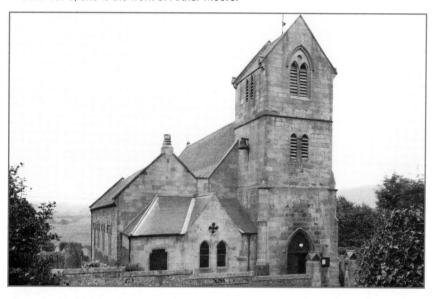

▼ Bamburgh, The Church c1960 B547031

A beam on the tower ceiling has been connected with the legend of the death of St Aidan, to whom the church is dedicated. Inside there is an effigy of Grace Darling made in 1844. There is also a part of a column with an inscription to the memory of the Reverend John Mackenzie, who was on the steamship 'Pegasus' when it was wrecked.

▲ Wooler, The Cross, the Church and the War Memorial c1955
W396001

The church of St Mary is one of the oldest buildings in the area - it dates from 1765. The cross has gone, sad to say, and there is now a green area where it stood. The shop that was Rutherford's the druggist's is now a beautician. Wooler was once a busy market town in the Middle Ages, and it saw frequent raids between the Scots and the English.

◄ **Berwick-upon-Tweed Distant View c1960**

B305046

Built to replace an earlier wooden bridge higher up the river, this beautiful sandstone bridge took almost fourteen years to complete. Finished in 1624 at a cost of £15,000, it comprises fifteen elegant arches. There are fourteen pillars, which are distinguishable by being slightly higher than the battlements.

Berwick-upon-Tweed, The Royal Tweed Bridge c1960 B305013
Designed by Mouchel and Partners, concrete engineers, and built in 1928, the Royal Tweed Bridge spans 428 metres. It is a concrete structure that was built to an iron bridge design. The street from the bridge leads into Marygate, and has spoilt the compactness of the area, unfortunately.

Holy Island, Lindisfarne Priory c1940 H348012
The remains of the church, with its weathered dark-red stone against a backdrop of the sea and fields, form a magnificent ruin. The priory was built in the early 12th century, but major restorations were carried out in the 1850s and in the early 20th century.

Castles and Buildings

Besides other many well-known battles, the county was also the scene of the longest-running feud in history. Starting in the reign of Edward I, and lasting 400 years, it continued until 1707 when the Union of Parliaments took place between England and Scotland. The legacies from this feud are the many castles, bastles and pele towers that were built at strategic points to withstand invasion. The bastles were fortified farmhouses. Animals would be kept on the ground floor, and humans would use the floor above. They were usually rectangular buildings with slits but no windows. The first floor was entered through a door in one of the gables, and the second floor had a similar door which was reached by a wooden ladder. Later the ladders gave way to stone steps. The pele towers were originally built of wood, and later were rebuilt in stone. These were usually smaller than a bastle. The first castles were also built in wood, but eventually these too were replaced by stone buildings. Many are now in ruins, but they still give some idea of the magnificence of the structures when they were complete. Dunstanburgh Castle was built in the 14th century; the largest castle in the county, it was only lived in for 150 years. Badly damaged during the Wars of the Roses, it was never repaired, and is now a magnificent ruin atop 100ft-high cliffs overlooking Embleton Bay. Bamburgh Castle stands on the site from which Anglo-Saxon kings once ruled Northumbria. The present castle, a Norman stronghold, dates from the 11th century.

During the Wars of the Roses it was damaged and went into decline. Restoration was carried out in the 18th century, and then again in the 19th century by Lord Armstrong, a Victorian engineer and industrialist. Ford Castle was restored in the 18th and 19th centuries. Owned by Lord Joicey, it is now used as a county and cultural education centre.

Lindisfarne was built as a Tudor fort to keep the Scots at bay, but it never saw any action. In 1903 it was bought by Edward Hudson and converted to a private dwelling by the architect Edward Lutyens. Alnwick Castle was built as a border fortress in the 11th century. Still lived in by the Percy family, it houses one of the best private art collections in Britain. The present castle was restored in the late 19th century, and it owes most of its present-day appearance to Anthony Salvin. He pulled down the earlier modifications carried out in 1755 by Robert Adam, and returned the building to a medieval-style one. When carrying out his work, he could never have foreseen that the castle would be used as the location to depict Hogwart's School of Witchcraft and Wizardry in a 21st century Harry Potter movie.

In buildings as old as these, there has to be the legend of a ghost or two, of course. In a room in the basement of Bamburgh Castle was a very deep well. At the bottom of the well, a wicked queen (who changed her stepdaughter into a worm) resides in the form of a toad. Every seven years she is supposed to reappear. Chipchase

Castle is reputedly haunted by the ghost of Sir Reginald Fitz-Urse, who was starved to death in the prison there. Dunstanburgh is haunted by a knight, Sir Guy. His anguished cries are said to be heard as he tries to find a way to enter the castle in pursuit of a lovely lady who lives there. Besides the monuments to battles, many other fine buildings remain that were built for a variety of uses, including quaint public houses, schools, town halls, hospitals and many others. Some still serve their original purpose, while others have become private residences, and many are now open to the public as museums.

Haltwhistle
Memorial Park and the Hospital c1960 H344049
Catering mainly for the elderly, the hospital still serves the needs of the public - it is the only hospital in Haltwhistle. It has been extended since this photograph was taken. The memorial to the men who lost their lives in the two World Wars still stands proudly in the same position.

Corbridge, The Angel Inn c1955 C459003
This charming building has a 17th-century core and Georgian and later alterations. The market place has two market crosses, one from the 13th century and one bearing the Percy crescent, which was presented in 1814. Many of what are shops now would have once been terraced houses.

Corbridge, Dilston Castle and the Chapel c1955 C459009
The estates once belonged to the Earls of Derwentwater. The last Earl was executed for his part in the 1715 rebellion. When his son died a few years later, the estate passed to the Greenwich Hospital Trustees, who demolished the hall and left the tower roofless. The chapel was built in the 17th century in the Tudor style.

▼ **Branch End, The Dr Syntax, New Ridley c1960** B546008
There are no hotels in the centre of Stocksfield. This public house is in New Ridley
and the Bluebells is in Mount Pleasant, quite a walk from the centre to both of
them. The Greek meaning of the word Syntax is 'to put words in order' - I wonder if
the customers can do that after a few pints.

▼ **Cornhill, The Collingwood Arms, the Garden c1955** C457011
The pretty, well-manicured garden with a lovely rose-bed belongs to
the early 19th-century coaching inn.

▲ **Wylam, Castle Hill
Convalescent Home
c1950** W397004
Built in 1878 as a family
home by Archibald Dunn,
a famous architect, it
changed hands in 1900.
The house was given to
the RVI in 1933, and
from 1937, until about
1988, it was used as a
convalescent home. The
building has now been
converted into flats, and
the surrounding land is a
housing development.

Otterburn, The Hall c1955 084003

Lord James Murray built this neo-Elizabethan house in 1869. The east front was altered in 1905, and after a fire in 1930 the interior was remodelled. To the rear of the hall there is a large conservatory. The building is now used as a hotel.

Bellingham, Brown Rigg Camp School c1960 B552009
In use as a boarding school for many years, Brown Rigg Camp School closed in the early 1980s. Some of the dormitories and classrooms remain, now converted into houses, but most of the area is now a caravan park. There is also a base here for pony trekking.

◀ **Newbrough
The Women's Institute
c1955** N201003
The Institute was
established in 1848, and
this building was erected
by subscription a few
years later. George J
Cookson enlarged the
premises in 1890. A
vending machine stands
outside on the pavement,
not a sight you would see
nowadays. Further down
the street is Nicholson's
provision store.

▼ **West Woodburn, The Bay
Horse Hotel c1955** W394005
Built in mellowed sandstone,
this charming 18th-century
coaching inn still serves the
public with their favourite
tipple. The inn stands near a
stone bridge on the River
Rede. Legend has it that at the
Battle of Otterburn in 1388,
the blood of the fallen stained
the river red, so giving it the
name Rede.

◀ **Acomb, The Youth
Hostel c1955** A250004
Owned by the Youth
Hostel Association, these
stables have been
converted into
reasonably priced, basic
accommodation, mainly
for backpackers and
walkers. There are two
sixteen-bed rooms and
one four-bed room.
There is also a
communal room and a
kitchen for self-catering.

Belsay, The Hall and the Stables c1955 B554005
Sir Charles Monck built the hall between 1807 and 1817 in the Greek Doric style, which was almost unknown in Britain at the time. The material used was sandstone with small pieces of iron ore, which give it a flecked appearance. The grounds were landscaped in the 18th century.

Morpeth, The Court House c1955 M251019
A family out for a stroll are walking away from the gateway that led to the gaol, which was demolished in 1891. The castellated Gothic court house was built between 1822 and 1828. The interior boasts an imposing staircase leading to a semi-circular courtroom and a vaulted passage through to the rear yard.

Morpeth, The Clock Tower c1965 M251084
Standing in the middle of Oldgate, it is apparently rare in England
for a belfry to stand on its own like this. It is believed it was erected
with reused materials in the 17th century. The top floor was added
on in 1705. To the left of the tower is the Grey Bull Hotel.

◄ **Mitford, The Castle c1955** M254001
These ruins have an interesting history. The original castle would have covered the whole summit of the mound. It was occupied by William the Lion in 1175, and by the Scots in 1318, when it was damaged irreparably. An excavation carried out in the early 20th century exposed graveyard monuments, but vandals later destroyed most of these.

◄ **Mitford, The Post Office c1955** M254006
This has been a village shop; here, if you bought an ounce of 'baccy', you would get a clay pipe free. It has also served as a tea-rooms and post office. As with many of these village shops, it lost out to the supermarkets, and is now a holiday home.

▼ **Shilbottle, The Farrier's Arms c1955** S518003
Of the three public houses that once served this mining community, this is the only one that remains. The gentlemen seem quite happy to have left their pints while they pose for the photograph. The billboard at the doorway reads 'Get your Eldorado ice-cream here'.

◄ **Alnwick, The Barbican 1881** 13972
This gateway was erected in the very early 14th century as a vantage point to monitor those who entered the castle grounds and as a means of defence against invasion. Originally there was a ditch, and a drawbridge was used as access. The figures keeping watch from the battlements are 18th-century soldiers, probably replacing earlier statues.

Alnwick, Alnwick Castle 1881 13973 Capability Brown designed much of the seven acres of landscaped grounds in about 1765. The castle stands flanked on one side by the River Aln and on the other by a ravine that was once Bow Burn. There have been many additions to the building over the centuries, but the original stone walling probably dates from the middle of the 12th century.

Craster, The Tower c1950 C352020
There is a record of 1415 listing this building, which suggests that it was originally medieval. It has, however, been thoroughly remodelled since then. The house to the front of the tower was built in 1769. In the 18th century, alterations were carried out in the Gothic style.

Craster, Dunstanburgh Castle 1951 C352011
Here we see the haunting ruins of what was once a magnificent building occupying eleven acres of land. It was well protected by nature on three sides; to the north were sheer cliffs, which made this an ideal site to build a fortress. The castle had a barbican, a gatehouse and three towers.

Wooler, The Black Bull Hotel c1955 W396033
In 1863, patrons of the Black Bull saw flames leaping from the
Three Half Moons opposite. The villagers used poles to pull thatch
from the roofs to beat at the flames. When the fire service arrived
several hours later, the flames were under control. The inn was
destroyed, and there was a lot of damage to other properties, but
the Red Lion and the Black Bull survived.

Wooler, The Cottage Hotel c1965 W396031
Dating back to the 17th century, the inn was used as a local excise office in 1837. In 1841 it was a post house for the London to Edinburgh route, a journey of 44 hours. When the Earl of Tankerville could not accommodate all his guests at Chillingham Castle, they would stay here - so the inn is now known as the Tankerville Arms.

Embleton, The Dunstanburgh Castle Hotel c1960 E150041
Once the site of a Quaker meeting house in the 17th century, part of the current building was a public house by 1828. After a few name changes and building additions, it had become a hotel by the early 20th century. The lovely old water pump and the telephone box have survived.

Beadnell, The Beadnell Towers Hotel c1955 B550040
The oldest part of this building was a granary in the 17th century. It then became a private residence, and was added to in the 19th century. In the 20th century it was owned by one of the founders of ICI Chemicals. Between the wars it became a hotel, and after the Second World War a country club. It is now back in use as a hotel.

**Bamburgh
The Castle c1955**
B547017
Bamburgh Castle is
situated on the Whin
Sill, and extensive views
of Holy Island can be
seen from here. The
medieval buildings were
in ruins when they were
sold to the Bishop of
Durham, Lord Crewe, in
1704. In 1757, a trustee
of the Crewe estate
began restorations. It
was further restored in
the late 19th and early
20th centuries.

Milfield, The School, the Chapel and the Manse c1960 M325013
While the three buildings have survived, the little school has not seen pupils in its classrooms since a new school was built and opened in 1963. However, because of a lack of funds, a kitchen was not added to the new building, and the meals are still cooked in the old building. The buildings have changed very little over the years.

Ford, The Castle Portcullis c1950 F207008
A magnificent castellated gateway and walls front an equally impressive castle. The portcullis dates from 1791-95. The building became an outdoor centre in 1991.

Ford, The School c1950 F207003
The Marchioness of Waterford built the Victorian Tudor
building in 1860 to be used as a school. The roundels on the
gables are inscribed with the date and the Waterford crest.
Inside are biblical scenes that were painted over a period of
twenty-one years by Lady Waterford for the children. Lady
Waterford Hall is now open to the public.

Holy Island, The Castle c1955 H348112
Lindisfarne was built about 1550 as a fort. It was used for this purpose until 1819. Edward Hudson, the owner of Country Life, bought the castle in 1902. The interior was in ruins, and he employed the architect Edwin Lutyens to convert the castle. This conversion was carried out with great sensitivity to the older parts of the building, and is a great success.

Farne Island, The Longstone Lighthouse c1960 F152002
This distinctive red and white lighthouse was built in 1826
and enlarged in the 19th century. It was manned for 160
years before giving way to modern technology and becoming
disused. It was the home of Grace Darling and her family at
the time when they carried out her famous rescue.
Unfortunately, it is not open to the public.

Wark, Chipchase Castle c1965 W393042
The chapel on the right of the view was rebuilt after 1735. The
interior has fluted Ionic pilasters and beautiful 18th-century
furnishings. The large house is Jacobean, dated 1621. The building
has been altered and modified over the centuries in keeping with
the fashions of the day.

Index

Frith Book Co Titles

www.francisfrith.co.uk

The Frith Book Company publishes over 100 new titles each year. A selection of those currently available are listed below. For latest catalogue please contact Frith Book Co.

Town Books 96 pages, approx 100 photos. County and Themed Books 128 pages, approx 150 photos (unless specified). All titles hardback laminated case and jacket except those indicated pb (paperback)

Title	ISBN	Price
Amersham, Chesham & Rickmansworth (pb)		
	1-85937-340-2	£9.99
Ancient Monuments & Stone Circles	1-85937-143-4	£17.99
Aylesbury (pb)	1-85937-227-9	£9.99
Bakewell	1-85937-113-2	£12.99
Barnstaple (pb)	1-85937-300-3	£9.99
Bath (pb)	1-85937419-0	£9.99
Bedford (pb)	1-85937-205-8	£9.99
Berkshire (pb)	1-85937-191-4	£9.99
Berkshire Churches	1-85937-170-1	£17.99
Blackpool (pb)	1-85937-382-8	£9.99
Bognor Regis (pb)	1-85937-431-x	£9.99
Bournemouth	1-85937-067-5	£12.99
Bradford (pb)	1-85937-204-x	£9.99
Brighton & Hove(pb)	1-85937-192-2	£8.99
Bristol (pb)	1-85937-264-3	£9.99
British Life A Century Ago (pb)	1-85937-213-9	£9.99
Buckinghamshire (pb)	1-85937-200-7	£9.99
Camberley (pb)	1-85937-222-8	£9.99
Cambridge (pb)	1-85937-422-0	£9.99
Cambridgeshire (pb)	1-85937-420-4	£9.99
Canals & Waterways (pb)	1-85937-291-0	£9.99
Canterbury Cathedral (pb)	1-85937-179-5	£9.99
Cardiff (pb)	1-85937-093-4	£9.99
Carmarthenshire	1-85937-216-3	£14.99
Chelmsford (pb)	1-85937-310-0	£9.99
Cheltenham (pb)	1-85937-095-0	£9.99
Cheshire (pb)	1-85937-271-6	£9.99
Chester	1-85937-090-x	£12.99
Chesterfield	1-85937-378-x	£9.99
Chichester (pb)	1-85937-228-7	£9.99
Colchester (pb)	1-85937-188-4	£8.99
Cornish Coast	1-85937-163-9	£14.99
Cornwall (pb)	1-85937-229-5	£9.99
Cornwall Living Memories	1-85937-248-1	£14.99
Cotswolds (pb)	1-85937-230-9	£9.99
Cotswolds Living Memories	1-85937-255-4	£14.99
County Durham	1-85937-123-x	£14.99
Croydon Living Memories	1-85937-162-0	£9.99
Cumbria	1-85937-101-9	£14.99
Dartmoor	1-85937-145-0	£14.99
Derby (pb)	1-85937-367-4	£9.99
Derbyshire (pb)	1-85937-196-5	£9.99
Devon (pb)	1-85937-297-x	£9.99
Dorset (pb)	1-85937-269-4	£9.99
Dorset Churches	1-85937-172-8	£17.99
Dorset Coast (pb)	1-85937-299-6	£9.99
Dorset Living Memories	1-85937-210-4	£14.99
Down the Severn	1-85937-118-3	£14.99
Down the Thames (pb)	1-85937-278-3	£9.99
Down the Trent	1-85937-311-9	£14.99
Dublin (pb)	1-85937-231-7	£9.99
East Anglia (pb)	1-85937-265-1	£9.99
East London	1-85937-080-2	£14.99
East Sussex	1-85937-130-2	£14.99
Eastbourne	1-85937-061-6	£12.99
Edinburgh (pb)	1-85937-193-0	£8.99
England in the 1880s	1-85937-331-3	£17.99
English Castles (pb)	1-85937-434-4	£9.99
English Country Houses	1-85937-161-2	£17.99
Essex (pb)	1-85937-270-8	£9.99
Exeter	1-85937-126-4	£12.99
Exmoor	1-85937-132-9	£14.99
Falmouth	1-85937-066-7	£12.99
Folkestone (pb)	1-85937-124-8	£9.99
Glasgow (pb)	1-85937-190-6	£9.99
Gloucestershire	1-85937-102-7	£14.99
Great Yarmouth (pb)	1-85937-426-3	£9.99
Greater Manchester (pb)	1-85937-266-x	£9.99
Guildford (pb)	1-85937-410-7	£9.99
Hampshire (pb)	1-85937-279-1	£9.99
Hampshire Churches (pb)	1-85937-207-4	£9.99
Harrogate	1-85937-423-9	£9.99
Hastings & Bexhill (pb)	1-85937-131-0	£9.99
Heart of Lancashire (pb)	1-85937-197-3	£9.99
Helston (pb)	1-85937-214-7	£9.99
Hereford (pb)	1-85937-175-2	£9.99
Herefordshire	1-85937-174-4	£14.99
Hertfordshire (pb)	1-85937-247-3	£9.99
Horsham (pb)	1-85937-432-8	£9.99
Humberside	1-85937-215-5	£14.99
Hythe, Romney Marsh & Ashford	1-85937-256-2	£9.99

Available from your local bookshop or from the publisher

Frith Book Co Titles (continued)

Ipswich (pb)	1-85937-424-7	£9.99	St Ives (pb)	1-85937415-8	£9.99
Ireland (pb)	1-85937-181-7	£9.99	Scotland (pb)	1-85937-182-5	£9.99
Isle of Man (pb)	1-85937-268-6	£9.99	Scottish Castles (pb)	1-85937-323-2	£9.99
Isles of Scilly	1-85937-136-1	£14.99	Sevenoaks & Tunbridge	1-85937-057-8	£12.99
Isle of Wight (pb)	1-85937-429-8	£9.99	Sheffield, South Yorks (pb)	1-85937-267-8	£9.99
Isle of Wight Living Memories	1-85937-304-6	£14.99	Shrewsbury (pb)	1-85937-325-9	£9.99
Kent (pb)	1-85937-189-2	£9.99	Shropshire (pb)	1-85937-326-7	£9.99
Kent Living Memories	1-85937-125-6	£14.99	Somerset	1-85937-153-1	£14.99
Lake District (pb)	1-85937-275-9	£9.99	South Devon Coast	1-85937-107-8	£14.99
Lancaster, Morecambe & Heysham (pb)	1-85937-233-3	£9.99	South Devon Living Memories	1-85937-168-x	£14.99
Leeds (pb)	1-85937-202-3	£9.99	South Hams	1-85937-220-1	£14.99
Leicester	1-85937-073-x	£12.99	Southampton (pb)	1-85937-427-1	£9.99
Leicestershire (pb)	1-85937-185-x	£9.99	Southport (pb)	1-85937-425-5	£9.99
Lincolnshire (pb)	1-85937-433-6	£9.99	Staffordshire	1-85937-047-0	£12.99
Liverpool & Merseyside (pb)	1-85937-234-1	£9.99	Stratford upon Avon	1-85937-098-5	£12.99
London (pb)	1-85937-183-3	£9.99	Suffolk (pb)	1-85937-221-x	£9.99
Ludlow (pb)	1-85937-176-0	£9.99	Suffolk Coast	1-85937-259-7	£14.99
Luton (pb)	1-85937-235-x	£9.99	Surrey (pb)	1-85937-240-6	£9.99
Maidstone	1-85937-056-x	£14.99	Sussex (pb)	1-85937-184-1	£9.99
Manchester (pb)	1-85937-198-1	£9.99	Swansea (pb)	1-85937-167-1	£9.99
Middlesex	1-85937-158-2	£14.99	Tees Valley & Cleveland	1-85937-211-2	£14.99
New Forest	1-85937-128-0	£14.99	Thanet (pb)	1-85937-116-7	£9.99
Newark (pb)	1-85937-366-6	£9.99	Tiverton (pb)	1-85937-178-7	£9.99
Newport, Wales (pb)	1-85937-258-9	£9.99	Torbay	1-85937-063-2	£12.99
Newquay (pb)	1-85937-421-2	£9.99	Truro	1-85937-147-7	£12.99
Norfolk (pb)	1-85937-195-7	£9.99	Victorian and Edwardian Cornwall	1-85937-252-x	£14.99
Norfolk Living Memories	1-85937-217-1	£14.99	Victorian & Edwardian Devon	1-85937-253-8	£14.99
Northamptonshire	1-85937-150-7	£14.99	Victorian & Edwardian Kent	1-85937-149-3	£14.99
Northumberland Tyne & Wear (pb)	1-85937-281-3	£9.99	Vic & Ed Maritime Album	1-85937-144-2	£17.99
North Devon Coast	1-85937-146-9	£14.99	Victorian and Edwardian Sussex	1-85937-157-4	£14.99
North Devon Living Memories	1-85937-261-9	£14.99	Victorian & Edwardian Yorkshire	1-85937-154-x	£14.99
North London	1-85937-206-6	£14.99	Victorian Seaside	1-85937-159-0	£17.99
North Wales (pb)	1-85937-298-8	£9.99	Villages of Devon (pb)	1-85937-293-7	£9.99
North Yorkshire (pb)	1-85937-236-8	£9.99	Villages of Kent (pb)	1-85937-294-5	£9.99
Norwich (pb)	1-85937-194-9	£8.99	Villages of Sussex (pb)	1-85937-295-3	£9.99
Nottingham (pb)	1-85937-324-0	£9.99	Warwickshire (pb)	1-85937-203-1	£9.99
Nottinghamshire (pb)	1-85937-187-6	£9.99	Welsh Castles (pb)	1-85937-322-4	£9.99
Oxford (pb)	1-85937-411 5	£9.99	West Midlands (pb)	1-85937-289-9	£9.99
Oxfordshire (pb)	1-85937-430-1	£9.99	West Sussex	1-85937-148-5	£14.99
Peak District (pb)	1-85937-280-5	£9.99	West Yorkshire (pb)	1-85937-201-5	£9.99
Penzance	1-85937-069-1	£12.99	Weymouth (pb)	1-85937-209-0	£9.99
Peterborough (pb)	1-85937-219-8	£9.99	Wiltshire (pb)	1-85937-277-5	£9.99
Piers	1-85937-237-6	£17.99	Wiltshire Churches (pb)	1-85937-171-x	£9.99
Plymouth	1-85937-119-1	£12.99	Wiltshire Living Memories	1-85937-245-7	£14.99
Poole & Sandbanks (pb)	1-85937-251-1	£9.99	Winchester (pb)	1-85937-428-x	£9.99
Preston (pb)	1-85937-212-0	£9.99	Windmills & Watermills	1-85937-242-2	£17.99
Reading (pb)	1-85937-238-4	£9.99	Worcester (pb)	1-85937-165-5	£9.99
Romford (pb)	1-85937-319-4	£9.99	Worcestershire	1-85937-152-3	£14.99
Salisbury (pb)	1-85937-239-2	£9.99	York (pb)	1-85937-199-x	£9.99
Scarborough (pb)	1-85937-379-8	£9.99	Yorkshire (pb)	1-85937-186-8	£9.99
St Albans (pb)	1-85937-341-0	£9.99	Yorkshire Living Memories	1-85937-166-3	£14.99

See Frith books on the internet www.francisfrith.co.uk

FRITH PRODUCTS & SERVICES

Francis Frith would doubtless be pleased to know that the pioneering publishing venture he started in 1860 still continues today. A hundred and forty years later, The Francis Frith Collection continues in the same innovative tradition and is now one of the foremost publishers of vintage photographs in the world. Some of the current activities include:

Interior Decoration

Today Frith's photographs can be seen framed and as giant wall murals in thousands of pubs, restaurants, hotels, banks, retail stores and other public buildings throughout the country. In every case they enhance the unique local atmosphere of the places they depict and provide reminders of gentler days in an increasingly busy and frenetic world.

Product Promotions

Frith products are used by many major companies to promote the sales of their own products or to reinforce their own history and heritage. Frith promotions have been used by Hovis bread, Courage beers, Scots Porage Oats, Colman's mustard, Cadbury's foods, Mellow Birds coffee, Dunhill pipe tobacco, Guinness, and Bulmer's Cider.

Genealogy and Family History

As the interest in family history and roots grows world-wide, more and more people are turning to Frith's photographs of Great Britain for images of the towns, villages and streets where their ancestors lived; and, of course, photographs of the churches and chapels where their ancestors were christened, married and buried are an essential part of every genealogy tree and family album.

Frith Products

All Frith photographs are available Framed or just as Mounted Prints and Posters (size 23 x 16 inches). These may be ordered from the address below. From time to time other products - Address Books, Calendars, Table Mats, etc - are available.

The Internet

Already twenty thousand Frith photographs can be viewed and purchased on the internet through the Frith websites and a myriad of partner sites.

For more detailed information on Frith companies and products, look at these sites:

www.francisfrith.co.uk
www.francisfrith.com
(for North American visitors)

See the complete list of Frith Books at:
www.francisfrith.co.uk
This web site is regularly updated with the latest list of publications from the Frith Book Company. If you wish to buy books relating to another part of the country that your local bookshop does not stock, you may purchase on-line.

For further information, trade, or author enquiries please contact us at the address below:
The Francis Frith Collection, Frith's Barn, Teffont, Salisbury, Wiltshire, England SP3 5QP.
Tel: +44 (0)1722 716 376 Fax: +44 (0)1722 716 881 Email: sales@francisfrith.co.uk

See Frith books on the internet www.francisfrith.co.uk

TO RECEIVE YOUR FREE MOUNTED PRINT

Mounted Print
Overall size 14 x 11 inches

Cut out this Voucher and return it with your remittance for £2.25 to cover postage and handling, to UK addresses. For overseas addresses please include £4.00 post and handling. Choose any photograph included in this book. Your SEPIA print will be A4 in size, and mounted in a cream mount with burgundy rule line, overall size 14 x 11 inches.

Order additional Mounted Prints at HALF PRICE (only £7.49 each*)

If there are further pictures you would like to order, possibly as gifts for friends and family, purchase them at half price (no additional postage and handling required).

Have your Mounted Prints framed*

For an additional £14.95 per print you can have your chosen Mounted Print framed in an elegant polished wood and gilt moulding, overall size 16 x 13 inches (no additional postage and handling required).

---

* IMPORTANT!
These special prices are only available if ordered using the original voucher on this page (no copies permitted) and at the same time as your free Mounted Print, for delivery to the same address

---

Frith Collectors' Guild

From time to time we publish a magazine of news and stories about Frith photographs and further special offers of Frith products. If you would like 12 months FREE membership, please return this form.

Send completed forms to:
The Francis Frith Collection, Frith's Barn, Teffont, Salisbury, Wiltshire SP3 5QP

Voucher for **FREE** and Reduced Price Frith Prints

Picture no.	Page number	Qty	Mounted @ £7.49	Framed + £14.95	Total Cost
		1	**Free of charge***	£	£
			£7.49	£	£
			£7.49	£	£
			£7.49	£	£
			£7.49	£	£
			£7.49	£	£

Please allow 28 days for delivery	*** Post & handling**	**£2.25**
Book Title	**Total Order Cost**	**£**

Please do not photocopy this voucher. Only the original is valid, so please cut it out and return it to us.

I enclose a cheque / postal order for £ . . . .
made payable to 'The Francis Frith Collection'
OR please debit my Mastercard / Visa / Switch / Amex card
(credit cards please on all overseas orders)

Number . . . .

Issue No(Switch only) . . . . .Valid from (Amex/Switch) . . . .

Expires . . . . Signature . . . .

Name Mr/Mrs/Ms . . . .

Address . . . .

. . . .

Postcode . . . . Daytime Tel No . . . .

Email Address . . . .

Valid to 31/12/04

The Francis Frith Collectors' Guild
Please enrol me as a member for 12 months free of charge.

Name Mr/Mrs/Ms . . . .

Address . . . .

. . . .

. . . . Postcode . . . .

Would you like to find out more about Francis Frith?

We have recently recruited some entertaining speakers who are happy to visit local groups, clubs and societies to give an illustrated talk documenting Frith's travels and photographs. If you are a member of such a group and are interested in hosting a presentation, we would love to hear from you.

Our speakers bring with them a small selection of our local town and county books, together with sample prints. They are happy to take orders. A small proportion of the order value is donated to the group who have hosted the presentation. The talks are therefore an excellent way of fundraising for small groups and societies.

Can you help us with information about any of the Frith photographs in this book? .

We are gradually compiling an historical record for each of the photographs in the Frith archive. It is always fascinating to find out the names of the people shown in the pictures, as well as insights into the shops, buildings and other features depicted.

If you recognize anyone in the photographs in this book, or if you have information not already included in the author's caption, do let us know. We would love to hear from you, and will try to publish it in future books or articles.

Our production team

Frith books are produced by a small dedicated team at offices in the converted Grade II listed 18th-century barn at Teffont near Salisbury, illustrated above. Most have worked with the Frith Collection for many years. All have in common one quality: they have a passion for the Frith Collection. The team is constantly expanding, but currently includes:

Jason Buck, John Buck, Douglas Burns, Ruth Butler, Heather Crisp, Isobel Hall, Hazel Heaton, Peter Horne, James Kinnear, Tina Leary, Hannah Marsh, Sue Molloy, Kate Rotondetto, Dean Scource, Eliza Sackett, Terence Sackett, Sandra Sanger, Lewis Taylor, Shelley Tolcher, Clive Wathen and Jenny Wathen.